Unprotected

A Tactical Approach to Boxing, Business, and Life

Alan Santana

Foreword by Jack Reiss

First Edition

PAGE PUBLISHING, INC.
New York, NY

First originally published by Page Publishing, Inc. 2017

ISBN 978-1-64027-539-3 (Paperback)
ISBN 978-1-64027-540-9 (Digital)

Printed in the United States of America

Also by Alan Santana

Pulling a Rabbit Out of My Hat

To my father, Armando Santana,
and my manager, Earl Beebe,
who taught me that hard work and dedication
pay off in the end, no matter what.

To my wife of thirty-one years, who has stood by every crazy idea
and business venture that I have thought up. She has allowed me
the freedom to continue to be creative and adventurous to no end.

To my four wonderful children, Victoria, Austin, Andrew and
Aaron, whom I love and admire for the wonderful young adults
that you have become. I hope that this book inspires you all.
Love, Alan

Contents

Foreword

Jack Reiss

I have known Alan for a while, and I am aware of his passion for boxing, so it came as no surprise to me that he was writing a book to help a new generation of fighters. Since he presented this idea to me, I have realized that it is an idea whose time has come.

We are living in an age of fast changes in all modern sports, and the changes that are taking place are usually to ensure safety. For example, bare-knuckle fighting began in the rear of taverns in England. These fighters battled for as many as eighty rounds, trading blows to all parts of their bodies until one was too injured or too exhausted to get up and continue. Today we limit the number of rounds and regulate the size of the gloves and the weights of the fighters, all to prevent deaths or injuries.

Alan's book has been written from his own experience. His desire is to help prepare the new generation of fighters—or any modern athlete—to be better able to handle the journey from obscurity to perhaps stardom and retain control of their destinies.

This book is designed to help them survive throughout their careers and prepare them financially for when they hang up their gloves and have to fend for themselves outside of boxing.

Preface

I have written this quick reference guide with hopes of helping boxers, both young and old, to be able to educate themselves and gain knowledge to successfully manage the business side of boxing. I have also included segmented portions of the history of boxing. Over my many years in the sport, I have seen time and time again professional boxers who have made tens of thousands of dollars to millions of dollars and wound up broke at the end of their careers. Therefore, I felt that this book would at least give them a fighting chance to succeed in the business while not being taken advantage of by others.

This is also a manual that can be read by anyone who may be interested in the fundamental steps of going into business for themselves. I have laid out the basics for anyone to start a business, no matter what their background is or what sport they participate in. This is Boxing 101, the business side. It is designed to give the necessary protection and cover needed in the ever-changing, chaotic arenas of boxing, business, and life.

Prologue

It was a normal day in the summer of 1961 as my mother and father made their usual trip to the grocery store. The trip was occasionally bumpy as my father navigated his green Ford pickup through the winding roads of Los Angeles. The warm sun glistened on my mother, exposing her beautiful features and moderate baby bump—she was six months pregnant.

As my dad proceeded to make a soft left turn, the passenger door, not properly secure, flung open and my mother was thrown out of the truck to the ground. My father brought the truck to a screeching halt and rushed to her aid. She was treated at the scene for minor bruises, yet the incident led to my premature birth. There I was, unprotected, weighing in at a whopping one and a half pounds and ten inches in length. Thus, my first fight began. The days and weeks to come were very challenging. However, I continued to fight, and after one month in the hospital's preemie ward, I was strong enough to be taken home.

I recall my parents once told me that I was small enough at birth to fit inside a shoe box. My quick response was "Perhaps that's why I love shoes." Yet when I was finally carried out of the hospital and placed securely into the cab of my dad's truck, I was wrapped tightly in a blanket and wearing no shoes. My father drove carefully home. I had defeated my first opponent, and now I lay in wait, resting up for my forthcoming bout with life, the next worthy contender.

Introduction

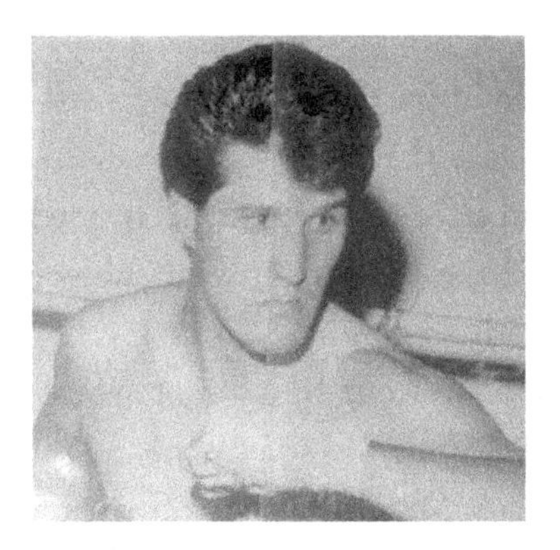

I put on my first pair of boxing gloves at the ripe old age of eight—I was a scrawny little kid who always got picked on in school, and I was tired of it. So I came home one day and asked my father to teach me how to defend myself. Unbeknownst to me, my father was a former professional boxer in his younger years, which I would find out years later when I set foot inside the 108th Street Gym. A trainer there said that I was the spitting image of my father, who was "a heck of a fighter back in his day." I discovered that Dad had finished his career with a 17–1 record, fighting out of Mexico and El Paso, Texas.

But on this day in 1969, my father took me to the local Big 5 Sporting Goods store in Long Beach, California, where he bought my first pair of boxing gloves (which now hang on my office wall). I was excited to learn the art of self-defense and could hardly wait to get started. Boxing came to me fairly easily. Learning how to throw a jab or put combinations together became as familiar and simple as tying my shoes. Dad was a paving contractor. He would come home after a long work day and spend time with me in our garage, teaching me everything he knew about the sport. After a few weeks, he would take me to Long Beach and have me run on the sand while wearing boots he had purchased for me at the local thrift shop.

We repeated this routine for at least three months, which seemed like a hundred years to me back then. My father also decided to start working with some of the kids in the neighborhood: James, Lewis, and Ronnie. Ronnie in particular was a big strong kid, the kind of kid that you made sure that you were friends with in case you ever got into trouble and needed backup. We trained for many months, learning to box and the ins and outs of the sport, until my father thought we were ready to compete.

He took us down to Long Beach, to the Seaside Gym. My childhood memory is of a dingy old smelly place. This is when I met the owner of the gym, Jake Shugrue, for the first time. Jake was a former Navy man with a wooden leg, due to an old injury while in the service. You would never see Jake without a fat cigar in his mouth. From that first day at the Seaside Gym, he always called me "Champ."

That night, I had my first boxing match. I won a decision over a kid from Long Beach who trained at Seaside. Ronnie, James, and Lewis would never fight again, even though each won his match. But that was my introduction into a great sport. Over the next twenty-seven years, I would have well over a hundred amateur fights and win many local boxing titles. I was trained by the late Bobby Chavez and Fabela Chavez. "The Great Fabela Chavez" left his mark on the sport fighting the top contenders in the 1940s and '50s. He made a lot of money fighting professionally, only to have it squandered by unscrupulous people who surrounded him. Over the forty-five years since I first walked into the Seaside Gym, I have met many ex-fighters, and a lot of them had stories of being taken advantage of in one way or another. Many had earned substantial sums in their heydays, only to find out at the end of their careers that the money was all gone.

It is still all too common to turn on the local or national news and hear about another professional athlete who has filed for bankruptcy, because he was overextended or made bad decisions or, even worse, was taken advantage of by a manager or business associate. When you are young, it seems like time stands still and money will last forever. But eventually we all get older and wiser and realize that money does not last forever unless you have a plan. I consider myself very fortunate to do what I do and to be involved with a sport that I truly love. My sincere hope is that you will find helpful the information I am about to share. The basic principles for success discussed in this book apply to all aspects of life, both personal and professional. As you pursue a career in boxing, business, or in higher education, the lessons that follow and skills that are discussed will help in your personal journey to success.

I wish you all the best!

Round 1

The History and Origins of Boxing

Boxing taught me the importance of research. When preparing for anything in life, especially if it is foreign subject matter, you must research and know the history. I tenaciously studied the sport I loved; I wanted to absorb as much information as I could. Boxing dates back more than five thousand years to the ancient Romans, Greeks, and Egyptians. If you look at ancient artwork, you will see drawings, paintings, and tile mosaics depicting the sport of boxing.

Boxing was introduced in the United States in the 1800s, brought over by the British and the Irish who were seeking a better way of life in the new world. Boxing in that day consisted of two men engaged in bare-knuckle fights that could last for several hours if neither man would quit. It was normal for fights to last thirty, forty, or even fifty rounds. People would place bets on the fighters, and the last man standing would be declared the winner. The longest fight in recorded history took place in 1893 and lasted for 111 three-minute rounds. In the end, the fight was called "no contest" because both fighters were too tired to come out of their corners. The fighters were Andy Bowen and Jake Burke. The decision was later changed to a draw.

The Marquess of Queensberry rules were introduced in 1867. This is considered the birth of modern boxing.

Boxing gloves were introduced, and three-minute rounds were established. This made the sport a bit less dangerous and, at the same time, gave it some legitimacy. However, bare-knuckle boxing continued well into the 1900s before being outlawed and going underground; it was still very popular in the United Kingdom until the 1970s.

To make fights more fair, weight classes were developed in the UK and the USA. The eight original weight classes were established, which are recognized worldwide:

- Flyweight—less than 112 pounds (50.8 kilograms)
- Bantamweight—up to 118 pounds (53.5 kg)
- Featherweight—up to 126 pounds (57.2 kg)
- Lightweight—up to 135 pounds (61.2 kg)
- Welterweight—up to 147 pounds (66.7 kg)
- Middleweight—up to 160 pounds (72.6 kg)
- Light-heavyweight—up to 175 pounds (79.4 kg)
- Heavyweight—over 175 pounds (79.4 kg)

The original weight classes were expanded in the 1960s when the World Boxing Conference (WBC) and the World Boxing

Association (WBA) split. This expansion made it easier for fighters to compete in different weight classes.

The WBC was formed in 1963 in Mexico City by then-President of Mexico Adolfo Lopez Mateos, and included eleven countries, including Mexico, the United States, and the United Kingdom. In 1983, for safety reasons, the WBC changed world title fights from fifteen to twelve rounds. You soon had four major sanctioning bodies: the WBC, WBA, World Boxing Organization (WBO), and International Boxing Federation (IBF). Today, even more bodies around the world sanction title fights in the respective weight classes.

The History Of Amateur Boxing In The USA

Boxing has become one of the most popular world sports. Amateur boxing was established as an organized sport around 1888. The rules of amateur boxing differ from those of professional boxing.

Amateur boxing was introduced into the Olympics in 1904. Since then, US boxers have won 111 gold medals. Many professional boxers were once a part of the Olympic boxing program and went on to win bronze, silver, and gold medals in international competition.

Sugar Ray Leonard may be the most recognized modern-era boxer to come out of Olympics and to do very well after entering the professional ranks. Leonard won gold in 1976 then went on to win professional world titles in various weight classes. He remains active within the sport today as a television commentator. Today's amateur program is still a stepping stone for fighters to move into the professional ranks in boxing in the hopes of winning a world championship. Wherever you live, you can go to local gyms and find that almost every single one is involved in the USA amateur boxing program.

Round 2

The Importance of Education

No matter what career path you decide to travel through, be it owning a business or working for a small or big company, or being a professional athlete, the key to your success is education.

Education can turn dreams into reality. An education can help you with decision-making, be it purchasing your first automobile, or being able to negotiate a contract with your manager or a promoter. Having good people skills will also be a big plus, and it all leads back to education.

Running Bay Cities, I have needed math skills for figuring out payroll, taxes, and deductions from the employees' checks.

Bookkeeping skills also came in handy, and knowing how to set up and run an office. As the years went by and my business grew, I was able to hire a staff to help run the office. This allowed me more time to be out in the field doing what I love to do, and that was meeting with potential new clients and running the job sites along with my employees. In any line of business, you run into problems, and having the knowledge and skills to think fast and make decisions while on the job site have always helped me through almost every problem that I have encountered. My math skills have come into play every time, and being able to calculate and figure out how much material will be needed for the job is very important in my line of work. You never want to order too much or not enough material for a job, because that could cost you time and money.

Education and Finances

It is well known that an education allows you to earn more money than a person who does not finish high school. Obtaining a degree from a junior college or a university will give you an advantage over someone who finishes high school and certainly over someone who has dropped out of high school.

A person who drops out of high school will earn an average of $19,000 a year. A person with a college degree will earn at least $1,000,000 or more over their lifetime. That is a very big spread in earnings.

Many professional athletes have made millions of dollars in their respective sports, only to wind up losing it all. In many cases, it was due to bad management of their personal finances or mishandling by paid management. You can look up many of these former professional athletes on the Internet by doing a Google search and read about their stories.

Dropout Rate of High School Students

The national high school dropout rate is around 7 percent. The rate for Hispanic students is around 13 percent as of 2014, which is far below the average of 32 percent in 2000. The dropout rate for black students is now around 8 percent, which is much lower than the rate of 15 percent in the year 2000.

During my boxing years, I continued to educate myself by reading and taking classes related to business in my chosen field and seeking hands-on training. This would help me out later in life when my career ended. I would wind up having ten professional fights over a two-year period, managed under the watchful eye of Earl Beebe, who himself was in the sport for over fifty years. I was promoted by John Ellis, who was also a professional fighter in the 1970s.

Earl was very high on education and continued learning, no matter what one's age was. "Education will allow you to do many things in your life," he would always tell me. I spent many hours with Earl both in the gym and outside the gym and at family events where we would have many discussions about education and life in general.

I had always been mindful of everything that was going on around me while in the sport and kept mental notes, which were stored in my brain, over the next several years. My middle school years were spent at a military school in Long Beach:Southern California Military Academy, where I would learn discipline and get a good education, while wearing a military uniform. My high school years were spent at Carson High School, in Carson, California. After graduating, I had a brief stint at Los Angeles Harbor College before going on to local business school in Long Beach, where I honed my business skills. Then I went to a trade school in San Pedro, California, where I learned blueprint reading.

The Lasting Value of Learning

So, in closing, a person who achieves a higher level of education is much more likely to succeed in every aspect of life, from finances to marriage, and beyond. Make a difference in your life by striving to be the best that you can be by educating yourself.

As you can see by the statistics mentioned above, it is important to acquire an education by any means possible. After high school, you may want to look into a trade school or, if you choose to go to college, you can look into grants or you may receive a scholarship which will help you to pay for your education.

Grants and scholarships can come from the federal government, your local government, or from local nonprofit organizations like the Masons, or even from local businesses or many other sources. A scholarship is based upon how well you did in high school and is usually awarded to students who maintained a high grade-point average.

Our federal government has set up the largest form of student aid in the country, federally aided programs that come in the form of grants, loans, and work-study assistance programs. All these are available to qualified students attending eligible post-secondary institutions such as vocational schools, colleges, and graduate schools.

A college education is extremely important but can be a very costly investment in your future. I suggest that you take the time to educate yourself along with your parents, who will play a vital role in helping you put together all of the necessary paperwork to get through the process. A grant is free money that never has to be paid back, but you must maintain a specific grade-point average to continue to qualify for the money. In some cases, a grant may have to be paid back if you fail to meet certain standards or do not finish school. Make sure that you understand any limitations that may be placed on the repayment of a grant if you fail to meet the standards set forth by the federal government.

When you do your homework on where and how to apply for a grant or the many scholarships that are available, the path becomes a bit easier to travel. But remember that there are deadlines you must meet each year to receive these grants or scholarships.

Here are a few places that you can go to on the Internet to help you in your search for a grant or scholarship:

- Free applications for Federal Student Aid at (FAFSA) Federal Pell Grants (these do not have to be repaid)
- www.2.ed.gov/fund/grants
- www.fafsa.ed.gov
- www.fedmoney.org

Round 3

In the Fight

What does it take to become a professional boxer or athlete?

The odds of actually making it to the professional ranks in any sport are against you. More than five hundred thousand kids play basketball, and out of those kids who play the sport into their college years, only one in approximately 8,900 will be drafted out of high school into the NBA. One in approximately 500 will be drafted into the NBA from college. One of approximately 350 college football players is drafted into the NFL.

In the world of boxing, there are 17,000 to 20,000 professional boxers worldwide. How many of these fighters can actually make a decent living at the sport? Maybe 1 percent to 2 percent of the top fighters will earn between $20,000 to $30,000 a year from the sport.

While training at the 108th Street Gym in Los Angeles, I first truly understood that fighters were there to try and better their lives by boxing. They hoped to make a little money along the way to their dream of becoming a world champion. Or they were just trying to fight their way out of poverty. I met a gentleman by the name of Ike Williams, always dressed in a nice shirt, tie, and sport coat, who himself was a former lightweight champion of the world. Ike had well over 150 professional fights in the 1940s and '50s. He earned quite a bit of money only to be taken advantage of because he could not read or write. He told me that the inability to read and write was one of his biggest regrets in life and had cost him dearly. I found it rather sad that a man would be taken advantage of by those who were supposed to be there to guide and protect him. Yet I have seen all too often where a fighter would make really good money, only to wind up losing it to bad managers who would take the money and invest it on properties for themselves or just blow it. I heard these stories firsthand from these former boxers, and I have also heard of the same horror stories happening over and over again to today's professional boxers. This also happens to professional athletes in other sports, who went broke because they were taken advantage of or were frivolous with their money.

I have always told young kids who are looking to become professional boxers that first and foremost the most important thing is to get an education. The De La Hoyas and Mayweathers of the world are few and far between who actually make considerable amounts of money in the sport. And even of those that do, most will still have to work while in the sport or after their careers have ended. The reality is that most young boys and girls who get into this sport are looking for a better financial way of life, and boxing, in some cases, can do that for them, but the odds are not in their favor. So again that is why I keep emphasizing the importance of an education.

You will see at the end of my book on the last page where I have listed professional athletes who have made millions of dollars only to lose it all in the end.

Manager, Trainer, and Sports Agent

What is a manager?

A manager is your advisor to help you with decisions in business, fight contracts, and, in some cases, financial matters. His job is to negotiate the best deal that he can get you. He will help to take care of travel arrangements, if needed, through the promoter. He will make sure that lodging and meals are taken care of when traveling away from home for a fight.

What is a trainer?

A trainer will make sure that you are well-trained and prepared for an upcoming fight, be it professional or amateur. He will work with you on conditioning, making sure that you are at the right weight for your fight. It is his job to communicate with the manager and let him know how you are progressing with your training on a daily or weekly basis.

What is a sports agent?

In some cases, you may want to sign with a sports agent. A sports agent helps manage an athlete's career in boxing, baseball, football, or whatever sport that you might be involved with. The agent can also handle legal matters, bookings, negotiate contracts, and market you to potential sponsors like Nike, Coke, or McDonald's. You get the picture.

The sports agent's role is similar to that of a manager, but you will be required to pay the agent a percentage of any income that you take in while under contract to the agent. You are not required to have a lawyer when signing with a sports agent or a manager. It all depends on your relationship with the agent. But I strongly recommend hiring a lawyer to make sure that all the documents are completed properly.

Fees for Services

In most cases, a manager will get 33 percent of your purse and the trainer will get 10 percent. This is the average going rate in the state of California; it could vary in other states. In some instances, the manager will not take any money from you until your fight purse reaches a certain amount; that is something that you can discuss with your manager and trainer prior to signing any contracts. It is most important to make sure that any understandings are in writing, no matter what anyone tells you.

Make sure that the contract is legal and binding in the State of California, or whichever state you live in. Have it notarized by a licensed notary in the city that you live in. The cost is usually around $10 per document, and you must present a valid driver's license or ID.

This is where your education will help you in negotiating a contract or any other type of deal that you may run across. Too many boxers are taken advantage of because they either did not read a contract or did not understand the verbiage and, at the end of their careers, had nothing to show for all the hard work and time that was spent in the gym and on the road preparing for fights.

Actually, this applies to anyone who is entering into an agreement for any business venture or even a purchase agreement contract for services or goods. Remember, "education is the key" to success in any aspect of life.

The Importance of a Contract

What is a contract?

A contract varies from state to state, but it is a legal and binding document that is entered into by two parties. A contract will help avoid misunderstandings and miscommunication, which is fairly common when negotiating verbally.

Here is an example with (1) a manager and boxer or (2) a promoter and a boxer. Both parties will agree to the terms of the contract, and it will be signed by both parties. You may also have a contract with a sponsor for endorsement of a specific product. The same principle applies to all contracts no matter what the contract is for. Do not let anyone tell you any differently.

You might want to have the contract written up by a lawyer who knows the terminology and the ins and outs of writing a legal and binding document.

Why is a contract important?

A contract is designed to protect you from being damaged or harmed and will make sure that you make the transition from an amateur athlete to a professional athlete.

Some professional athletes will make more money in one year than most people make in a lifetime. A contract in sports is known as a "Personal Service Agreement" because of the athlete's unique abilities. It is very important to have a contract to protect you in case there are any problems down the road with management or even trainers.

What is a breach of contract? It is when you have entered into an agreement and one of the parties fails to uphold their end of the deal. Having a contract is a good way to do business, and it will save you lots of problems in the long run. People will try and get out of a contract for many reasons after the contract has been written, so make sure that you go over every aspect of the contract/agreement before you sign it, and make sure that you completely understand it. If you fail to abide by any of the terms of the contract, you would be in breach of a contract. The same rules apply for the management or adviser. They too must abide by the terms and conditions of the contract/agreement or else they are in breach of contract.

Medical/Health Exams

Why is a medical checkup important?

In every state, including California, it is required that you go to a licensed medical doctor who is approved by the state athletic commission for a physical prior to being granted a boxing license. Your health is the most important thing when participating in any sport, not just boxing.

You are required to have an annual physical when participating in both amateur and professional sports in the State of California. All medical records are kept on file with the local boxing commission.

The medical examination/checkup is a very important part of any physical activity, whether it be just working out on your own or participating in a physical sport. In most cases, you will not be given a clearance to fight if your medical records are not up to date.

Licensing as a Professional Athlete

It is a requirement that every person who participates in any contact sport in the State of California is licensed. Visit the California State Athletic Commission website at: http://www.dca.ca.gov/csac/

The website provides important information for all amateur and professional athletes, managers, and promoters, including forms and legal information.

You can find the same information for your city or state by looking it up on the Internet or checking your local business listings.

Round 4

The Business Side

It is important that every boxer have a fundamental knowledge of the business side of boxing. Additionally, I think all new fighters, and athletes in general, should take a mandatory financial planning course.

Below is a list of former World Champion Boxers who have filed for bankruptcy over the years. I have also included a few other professional athletes, because this sad phenomenon is not limited only to fighters.

- Mike Tyson, reportedly earned $350 million over his career
- Evander Holyfield, reportedly earned $250 million over his career
- Riddick Bowe, reportedly earned $50 million over his career

- Iran Barkley, reportedly earned $5 million over his career
- Joe Louis, reportedly earned $4.6 million over his career
- Latrell Sprewell (basketball) reportedly earned $100 million over his career
- Marion Jones (track), earned $80,000 per race
- Antoine Walker (basketball), reportedly earned $110 million over his career

As you can see, the list of celebrity sports stars who have gone broke over the years is amazing, and the list goes on and on and is being repeated time and time again. When will it stop? The amount of money that the professional athletes have earned is staggering, and they should have never wound up in these dire circumstances. Was it bad decision-making, bad management, or not educating themselves so that they would not wind up in this position? Hopefully this book will help you not to wind up in this position.

Starting a Business

Boxing is a business in itself, but many athletes who are earning large sums may also want to start other businesses to have something to fall back on when their sports careers are over. Again, education is the key.

I educated myself in business and also absorbed everything that my father had taught me in my youth about being in business. He always instilled in me the value of working hard, no matter what you do, and that you can succeed in anything if you put your mind to it.

Many people start a business without knowing the hows, whats, and whys. I hope the information that I have put into this book will help you get started on the right foot. I focus on three of the main things that you will need to do to open up a business in most states. You should check with your local city hall for more information on what is needed.

I retired as a fighter in 1989 after having an accident while driving a dump truck to one of our job sites. I was told by my doctor that I could never fight again. That was a very hard blow for me, but fortunately, during the time while I was chasing my dreams of becoming a world champion, I had already started something to fall back on. I began Bay Cities Paving in 1989 and have been in the business now for well over thirty-four years. My company has provided a fairly good life for my family. I have also ventured into other businesses with friends and people that I met on my travels around the country and abroad.

Bay Cities Paving Company has been my main business for the past twenty-seven years, and throughout those years, I have experienced almost every situation that you can encounter in business.

I have found that having good people skills is a must when you are dealing directly with the public. Being a well-rounded and cultured person also helps. You will need many other skills when running your business or even when working as an employee for a company.

I have heard many young people say, "Why do I need to take that class? I will never use any of that knowledge in real life." You never know what curve ball you will be thrown, and often you will need to be a fast thinker and use life skills and education to help you along the way. Running a full-time business takes a lot of courage and the strong will to want to succeed in business. As I said earlier, find something that you are passionate about, be it a hobby or something that you really like doing; and in many cases, you can turn that into a business.

Filing a Fictitious Business Statement

Anyone seeking to start a business must start by filing a fictitious statement at your local newspaper office. This is a legal document known as a DBA or "doing business as." The purpose is to let people know that you are doing business as a legal owner. The cost to file this paperwork is about $100. It may vary from state to state.

A Business License

A business license is required when operating a business in any city. This is usually acquired after filing the paperwork for your "DBA" —fictitious business statement.

Why is a business license needed? A city business license is required because the city in which you operate is entitled to local taxes, usually based on the annual sales of your business and the type of business it is.

You can check with the finance office at your local city hall to find out about the fees associated with filing this paperwork.

Federal Tax ID

A federal tax ID number (also known as an FEIN) is required for doing business in the United States. This will help with the filing of business taxes and is needed when banking, opening some accounts, etc.

Banking and Insurance

Banking dates back to the 15th century in Italy and played a major role in the Italians' rise to global power.

A bank is a financial institution that is set up to take people's money for deposit and is licensed and regulated by the Unites States. Wells Fargo has been around since the 1850s and is arguably the most recognized bank in the United States. Here is a link on the history of Wells Fargo Bank: https://www.wellsfargo.com/about/history/adventure/since_1852

There are plenty of choices for banking. Find a local bank that works for you and that you are comfortable working with. Develop a working relationship with the manager and get to know them and allow them to get to know you. You will be able to discuss many options for your money while depositing it into the bank. Speak with a financial officer of the bank, set some time aside to meet with them, and ask questions on investing your money and what works for you.

Opening a Bank Account

When opening a personal bank account, you will need a Social Security number and a valid state ID or driver's license. If you are under eighteen, you will need a parent to open the account with you

For a business account, you will need a valid state ID or driver's license, a fictitious business statement (see above), a federal tax ID number, and, in some cases, a city business license.

Why an Insurance Policy?

Insurance has been around for hundreds of years and was first used by the Chinese to insure their goods while travelling across the vast oceans. Insurance policies date back to the third century BC. The first insurance company in the United States was started in 1732 in Charleston, South Carolina.

There are various types of insurance policies for various needs. An insurance policy is good to have in case of an accident that may end your career as a professional athlete or business owner. Protecting your most important assets is an essential step in creating a solid personal financial plan. The right insurance policies will go a long way toward safeguarding your earning power and your possessions.

When you take out an insurance policy on yourself, you will pay a monthly fee called a premium. If under contract with a manager or a management company, you may want to discuss having an insurance policy and the premiums being paid for by the manager or management company. You can contact your local insurance agency to discuss policies, pricing, and plans. Look under local business listings for an agent or on the Internet.

Round 5

Appearance Matters—Dressing for Success

A number of clothiers and boutiques around the country emphasize the importance of a nice suit. Fashion floods advertising nationally and internationally. The fact is that a great suit on a well-groomed man carries a lot of weight. Looking good makes a lasting impression, especially in the business world, where a person's physical appearance speaks volumes and could make the difference in being considered for great opportunities.

When I was fighting professionally, I realized pretty quickly that by dressing up in a nice suit and tie, I could set myself apart from every other fighter. To be noticed, I dressed as if I were going into the office for a business meeting. I was nicknamed "The Matinee

Idol." I was pulled aside many times at press conferences and asked to be interviewed and photographed. This led to my being invited on sports talk radio shows and getting a Hollywood agent. Being represented by George Jay then allowed me to get a taste of the acting bug and land some small television roles.

Dressing for success is an individual's choice, and the most important thing is to create your own look and style. You can always consult with an image consultant to help you find out what works for you. In today's world, and especially for professional athletes or even business owners, fashion is very important, and first impressions can make or break you. The NBA's Dwayne Wade is considered the best-dressed athlete in sports. He takes personal pride in his appearance while out in the public eye with his choice of fashion before and after the game.

Always look as neat as you can. I tell my employees that people will form an opinion within seconds of meeting you, so it is best to always be prepared to make that good first impression.

Dressing nicely does not have to be expensive. Many clothing discount stores offer brand-name suits for men. Purchase two or three different dress shirts, a couple of ties, and a nice pair of dress shoes.

Young women similarly have many options in fashion at reasonable prices. Purchase a couple of nice dresses, a basic suit or pantsuit, and always own a nice pair of shoes.

Remember that you are in business for yourself, and boxing is a business. You are creating a "brand." This is a good mindset to have going into this business. You will be taken much more seriously, and it will pay off in the long run—people will respect you more.

Make it a goal to be successful. Dress the part. Remember, "You are the Brand."

Round 6

Public Speaking

The ability to speak well in public will be a very important part of your overall package and establishing your "brand." Speaking confidently and intelligently will allow you to stand out in a crowd and to be noticed. Press conferences are common, and there will be many opportunities for interviews by local news media.

Most people have a fear of speaking in public. If you lack confidence in making comments to an audience, consider enrolling in public speaking classes at your local community college. Another opportunity for practice and mentorship is through Toastmasters International. This organization meets monthly in many cities. Visit www.toastmasters.org to find a group in your area.

Even without taking classes or joining a group, there are a few things that you can learn that will help when speaking in public or to groups of people.

Always make eye contact with your audience when speaking. Speak slowly and do not allow yourself to get into a race to finish your sentences. While speaking, most people will tend to speed up; this is a sure sign of being nervous. Always take a deep breath before you start to speak and allow yourself a moment to gain your composure.

Walk out onto the stage as if you own it, and show confidence while onstage that you are in control. If you project confidence while speaking, people will believe you. The most important thing to remember is that you are in control. Do not let your emotions get the best of you while onstage or in front of the cameras. When taking questions, make sure that you take a moment to think your answer through before you start speaking.

Be passionate about your topic. One of the things that I do before going out to any event that I will be speaking at or be the master of ceremonies of is to study my subject. Find out as much as you can about your subject from books or the Internet, then get to know your subject well. Really do your homework on your topic.

Take the time to prepare yourself mentally before you step out onstage in front of your audience. That is a key factor in being able to get your point across and to look like you really know what you are talking about. If you need to, stop and take a drink of water and compose yourself before moving on. Let your audience see you who are by being at ease while up onstage. It will show, and you will win them over by being yourself.

There have been times when I would find myself all tied up in knots prior to speaking. What I did was to put my mind in a place where I could relax. I would visualize myself up onstage in front of everyone and being in control of my emotions.

One of the advantages that I have is all of my years of training as a boxer. I compare preparing for public speaking to preparing for an upcoming fight. It is a frame of mind, and if you can keep yourself in check, you will do just fine.

A little nervousness, however, is not to be feared. I have hosted many events over the years, and I find that as each event is finished and I move on to the next one, I still have the same butterflies that I did the very first time that I stepped out onto the stage.

The first time that I did that, I was working in the network marketing business with my business partner, Eric Ratley. We would go to the venue that we were going to speak at and set everything up, from the computer to the loudspeakers. I found myself really nervous the first time that I was going to go out and speak to about thirty people who had come out to see what we were selling.

Needless to say, I survived and went on to do many speaking events all across the country and had some success at it. After a while, I found myself walking out and not even thinking about the butterflies, as it all fell into place. The one thing that I did learn is that we are all the same in the end, and there is really nothing to be nervous about. Remember, "just be yourself," and you will be fine.

You will always want to end by saying, "Thank you."

Round 7

Anatomy of a Promoter

The first question that I would ask myself is "What is a promoter, and why do I need one?" Many boxers out there don't understand the infrastructure of promoting a fight. It is essential that fighters educate themselves as much as possible. Awareness is key, and it could help in fighters recognizing when the promoter or potential promoter is presenting a potentially bad opportunity. Now that I understand the intricacies of fight promotion, it has helped me to explain the details to other fighters in a clear and concise manner.

A promoter is someone who arranges events; boxing would fall under that category. A promoter is responsible for making the arrangements to secure a venue for the boxing card. It is the promoter's responsibility to sell tickets to the event, advertise the event, market the event, and, finally, to make sure that everything runs smoothly. Remember a promoter is not a manager—these are two completely different roles, which I will go into a little more detail in the next chapter.

A promoter's job is to pay for every aspect involved with the boxing card. This means that the promoter is taking on the financial responsibility for the entire event. In some cases, the promoter might use private investor money that has to be repaid after all of the purses are paid to the boxers for the event.

This is very important. I experienced the downside of this in Colorado when a boxing promoter promised that he would reimburse me for airfare for myself and my fighter, Christina Rodriguez.

In the end, we were not paid for the airfare or Christina's purse for the fight. I lost about $750. I did phone the State of Colorado to file a complaint against the promoter, but nothing was ever done, and we never received any money from this promoter. In fact, I found out that no one was paid for their services that night, and I was completely unaware of the insurance bond that was in place to protect me from a financial burden. This promoter never promoted another event in Colorado because of all of the complaints that were filed against his promotion company.

In every state, a boxing promoter is required to put up an insurance bond. This bond is to protect fighters and to make sure that they get paid. It also insures that everyone involved with the event is paid. You can ask the promoter to show you a copy of his insurance bond. It is a requirement of the athletic commission in the state that you will be fighting in. An insurance bond cost can range from $5,000 to $25,000 or more depending on the financial responsibility of the promoter. The bond is based on his business and personal credit history. At the end of the day, the bond is to make sure that the promoter does his job to insure the success of the event.

Without working with a local promoter, you more than likely will not be able to get fights on your own, and you will eventually have to sign a contract or agreement with the promoter. I discussed contracts earlier in the book.

Round 8

The Status of Boxing

Today, as I ponder the status of boxing, I have to really stop and think about what it was like for me in the 1980s when I fought as a professional under the ring name "The Matinee Idol."

Looking back, I was very fortunate to be introduced to Earl Beebe who would become my manager after I was introduced to him by my father, Armando. I was twenty-seven years old and had been told by many people who did not really know me that I was too old to fight professionally. Back in the day, twenty-seven was considered old for fighters in the featherweight division. I had a point to prove to these so-called boxing experts who were telling me that I was too old. What they did not realize is that I had been actively fighting in the amateurs over the last fourteen years and had not taken too much time off from the sport.

Even though I was twenty-seven, I looked much younger and felt great. My manager was more than fair to me when it came to how much money he would take from my purse—the reality was that he took nothing. I did not even have to pay the monthly dues for the gym where I trained.

My first professional fight took place in February 1988 and was televised on a Saturday night in the Los Angeles area.

I lost a split decision that everyone thought that I had won hands down; even the boxing commentator Armando Muniz thought that I was robbed and should have won a decision. That was my introduction to professional boxing. I carried myself as a professional even after hearing the raw decision that I was given.

We put it behind us and continued to move forward. My manager was soon approached by another fight promoter, John Ellis of South Bay Promotions, and we were soon fighting regularly on his shows in the Redondo Beach area. The one thing that we did was help the promoter sell tickets to our family and friends. For me, it was not a problem at all, and I was able to sell quite a few tickets, and we made a great deal with the promoter that we would get a percentage of the gate along with another boxer by the name of Rickey Romero.

Rickey and I were sparring partners in our amateur days while working out together at the Fabela Chavez Gym. We fought on several shows together and did well in our early careers. Rickey went on to have a very good career as a professional boxer in the flyweight division. He won the California title in the 118-pound class. As I mentioned earlier, my career was cut short due to an automobile accident in 1990.

The promoters that we worked with in the 1980s were a little more stand-up than a lot of the promoters that I see in today's game.

I have heard on several occasions that a local fight promoter will ask the trainer or manager to pay for his fighter and the opponent to be on a local show. That is completely against the law but is being done all over the country. I had a fighter come over from Italy. We went to the local gym to take a look at him, and in the end, we decided to keep him here for a while. I phoned a Texas promoter that I knew to see if we could get our fighter a ten-round tune-up bout, then maybe a title shot. I was told that it would cost us $14,000 to put our fighter on the card. Needless to say, that did not happen.

I have also heard of fighters' purses being withheld by the fight promoter for not selling enough tickets. This was brought to my attention a few months ago by a very good friend and business partner who works with me to sanction WBF title fights in Los Angeles. We have not had much luck due to the fact that the local fight promoter want the two combatants to put up the money to fight for the title. This goes against my standards, and I will not let that happen ever again under my watch as the North America coordinator for the WBF.

I once witnessed a referee being handed an envelope while in the dressing room with my fighter, Christina Rodriguez. Her trainer, Bill Slayton, witnessed the same thing. We kept quiet until we were on our way back to Los Angeles, when I had asked him if he saw what I saw. He confirmed that he saw the envelope being handed to the referee from a manager. So that goes to show you that you cannot trust anyone in the sport; there is so much corruption that goes on within the sport and is just kind of swept under the rug. No one ever talks about it due to the fear of being blackballed and being unable to fight again on some of these promoters' cards.

I truly feel that we really need a national boxing commission to oversee the state boxing commissions. The reason that I am saying that is because I have dealt with boxing commissions in many states only to find that they are completely incompetent and unable to handle the task in front of them. I was once asked by a boxing commission to run the entire weigh-ins and rules meetings because the commissioners were new and did not quite know what to do. I have witnessed a commissioner in Delaware completely overstep his boundaries and use his power for several years to bully managers, fighters, and staff just so he could keep total control over his position. He was being paid well by the state for his services, and it seemed to me that he was not well liked because of the way he let the power of his position get to him.

I went so far as to write a detailed letter to the president of the Dover Downs Casino about my experiences with this gentleman and how I truly felt that he needed to be removed from this position. He was eventually asked to step down and is currently being investigated by the federal government for his actions. This only strengthens my argument for a national boxing commission to oversee and regulate the sport in the entire country. Boxing is the only professional sport that does currently not have a national commissioner in place. Football, baseball, basketball, and hockey have commissioners. Only boxing has no national commissioner, just local commissioners who oversee their own jurisdictions.

There have been several attempts and discussions about a national commissioner, but to date, nothing has come of those talks. Below, I have included the Muhammad Ali Reform Act of 2000 so that you can become familiar with it. This law that was put in place by our Congress after some help from Senator John McCain, who is an advocate for the sport.

The Muhammad Ali Boxing Reform Act, commonly referred to as the Ali Act, is a federal law that was introduced in 1999 and enacted May 26, 2000, by the 106th Congress to (1) protect the rights and welfare of boxers; (2) aid state boxing commissions with the oversight of boxing; and (3) increase sportsmanship and integrity within the boxing industry [See 114 Stat. 321(3) (2000)]. The law amended the 1996 Professional Boxing Safety Act by expanding upon provisions against exploitation, conflict of interest, enforcement, and more.

The act was passed in response to widespread abuse of boxers by means of exploitation, rigged rankings, and rigged matches.

Congress noted through research that a number of problems with the sport needed to be addressed to ensure the safety and protection of professional boxers. Listed are a number of discoveries made by Congress [see 144 Stat. 322(3) (2000)]:

- Professional boxing is not governed by any league, association, or any form of an established organization like majority of other professional sports.
- The state officials are not ensuring the protection of the boxers and are not aware or informed of contracts boxers have agreed to.
- Promoters are taking advantage of the sport by conducting dishonest business affairs. Promoters are not being punished due to some states being less strict about the legal terms that are stated in contracts.
- There is no rating system provided to rank professional boxers thus ratings are subjected to manipulation by those in charge.
- There has been a major interference in the sport by because of open competition by restrictive and anti-competitive bodies.
- There are no restrictions placed on contracts that boxers agree to with promoters and managers. It is necessary to enforce a national contract reform which will guarantee the safety of professional boxers and the public from unlawful contracts and to enhance the integrity of the sport.

The act has been criticized for numerous reasons. First of all, it provides rules but leaves enforcement of these rules to the states, without defined guidelines. Also, some believe that Congress has no business regulating the boxing industry if it does not regulate any other sport.

This one-page summary of the Muhammad Ali Boxing Reform Act HR 1832, was posted in 2002 on Senator McCain's website:

> PROTECTION FOR BOXERS FROM COERCIVE CONTRACTS "Sense of the Congress" recommendation that the ABC should develop minimum guidelines for boxer contracts, and that state commissions should follow them. The Act imposes a one-year limit on promotional rights that a promoter forces a boxer (or the boxer's current promoter) to provide, in those situations where the boxer in question would otherwise be denied the opportunity to compete in a bout. i.e. "Unless you give me options on future bouts, you don't get this one." Any contractual rights thereby gained are limited to 1 yr. The Act prohibits any entity in boxing from forcing a mandatory challenger (such as a No. 1 ranked contender) to give up promotional rights, or otherwise be denied the mandatory bout. SANCTIONING ORGANIZATION REFORMS "Sense of the Congress" recommendation that the ABC should develop guidelines for the legitimate ranking of boxers, and that sanctioning organizations (SO's) should follow them. SO's must respond to protests from boxers about their rankings within 7 days. SO's must

provide a justification for changes they make in their "Top 10" rankings on their Internet website. On an annual basis, SO's must publicly disclose their ratings policies & bylaws; the fees they charge boxers; and the names & addresses of their members who decide rankings. The information must be provided either on their website or to the Federal Trade Commission. SO's must disclose all charges they impose on a boxer, and all sources of their revenue, to the supervising state commission. REQUIRED DISCLOSURES FOR PROMOTERS Promoters must fully disclose the following information to the supervising state commission: complete copy of their contracts with the boxer(s); all fees and charges they impose on the boxer(s); all payments made to SO's; any reduction in the purse promised to the boxer(s); advise the boxer of the revenues gained by the promoter from the event. Additionally, judges & referees must disclose payments received.

To participate in a bout, they must be certified by that state. CONFLICTS OF INTEREST Promoters are barred from having financial ties to the manager of a boxer. (exception provided for club show promoters) SO's are prohibited from receiving hidden payments from any source in the industry. ENFORCEMENT Individuals knowingly violating the Act can face up to one year in jail or fines up to $100,000. (Larger fines re: major events) State Attorneys General can initiate civil

> actions & injunctions under the Act. Boxers can bring private actions. MISCELLANEOUS PROVISIONS Each state boxing commission must enforce the suspension of boxers due to misconduct that are imposed by other state commissions. "Sense of the Congress" recommendation that state commissions should provide information to boxers about the risk of brain injuries in the sport. If a state does not have a boxing commission, boxing events held in that state may be supervised by representative of the A.B.C. State commissions shall renew boxer ID cards every four years.

As you can see by reading the Ali Act of 2002, boxing is in a complete state of disarray and truly needs someone to step up to the plate and do something about it. This is one of the richest sports in the world, and it has some of the biggest purses ever paid to boxers. Yet it is also one of the poorest of sports if you are on the other end of the spectrum.

Fighter will contend for purses of $800 or less for a four-round fight. When you put that into perspective, it would be much less than the national minimum wage for training. Fighters must train for at least a two- to three-month period to prepare for a fight, only to be paid $800 and then have a portion of the purse taken by their trainer and, in some instances, their manager, leaving them with less than half of the original purse.

Stop and think about that for a moment. Would you put your life on the line for that kind of money? That is something to think seriously about. That's why it is so important to educate yourself and your parents so that you do not wind up as one of the many professional athletes who are broke after it is all said and done.

Professional boxers also have no retirement plan or insurance policy in place while they are fighting. This has been another sore spot for both fighters and promoters.

This is another topic of discussion that has been discussed for over thirty years now only to still be talking about today. I truly feel that if we once again had a national commissioner that I would not be writing this book today. It is something that needs to be discussed and talked about until something is done about it on both a state and national level. These are issues that need to be brought to the attention of boxers and fans all over the country and the world. Until it is, I will continue to get the word out though this book or at local events that I host.

Round 9

Sanctioning the Sport

When you talk about sanctioning the sport today, my personal opinion is that there are way too many sanctioning bodies. I am currently the North American coordinator for the World Boxing Foundation, which is located in Australia and is one of the oldest sanctioning bodies in the world. The WBF was founded by Larry Carrier in 1988 in Bristol, Tennessee, under the name World Boxing Federation—of which I also was the North American Coordinator from 2011 to 2014. Because of problems, I resigned and moved over to the World Boxing Foundation and have been with them since August 2014.

There are currently the WBC, WBA, IBF, IBO, UBC, WBFed, WBFoundation, UBF, and the list goes on and on. For a list of sanctioning bodies, see https://en.wikipedia.org/wiki/List_of_boxing_organisations

As you can see, there are currently way too many boxing organizations around the world and here in North America to be taken seriously. The reason is money—everyone wants a piece of the action. Where does this end?

Again, I have to go back to the concept of bringing in a national boxing commission to oversee each state and to regulate the sport so that every fighter has an equal opportunity to make a decent living and maybe even become a world champion. Every boy and girl who sets foot inside a boxing gym dreams of becoming a world champion. I want to help educate them properly and to help them maybe achieve that goal of being a world champion. We need to be able to regulate the sanctioning bodies and keep them in check when it comes to the exorbitant fees and percentages that are taken away from the fighters purses.

The Pacquiao/Mayweather fights sanctioning body was trying to collect over $200,000 in sanctioning fees from both fighters for their last mega bout. In my personal professional opinion, sanctioning bodies should not be allowed to charge such high fees to sanction a title fight. On top of that, you still have to pay the judges and the referee for working the fight; so as you can see, the deck is totally and completely stacked against the fighters, and in the end, they really have no one to protect them. They are dealing with the promoters and the sanctioning body, and in some cases, more than one sanctioning body. If there is more than one title on the line, then the fighters have to pay those fees too.

As you can see, it is a very uneven playing field for boxers in today's world of promoters, managers, and trainers. Education is the key to not being put into these types of situations. By educating yourself, you gain the tools to make good decisions.

I have seen and witnessed how sanctioning bodies run the events from behind closed doors. As a supervisor, I have overseen well over ten title fights here and in Mexico over the past five years. I can tell you firsthand that I have witnessed things that should have not happened.

One Saturday night in Mexico, I was there to supervise a female world title fight between a boxer from Mexico and one from Taiwan. When I went in to check on the fighters' hand wraps, those of the fighter from Taiwan were completely wrong and could have caused serious damage to her opponent or to herself. I tracked down a trainer who rewrapped her hands properly, and I signed off on the hand wraps. In the end, the fight went off without a hitch.

The funny thing about this story is that I was not officially in charge of that particular fighters' room. It was under another sanctioning body that I will not mention.

On another occasion in Atlanta, I was also the sanctioning body supervisor to oversee the scoring of a fight along with the local boxing commissioner. The scoring was completely out of kilter with the three judges who were working the fight. I would never allow that judge to work another WBF title fight again.

As a coordinator/supervisor, it is my job to make sure that the scoring for a fight is in line and fair, and if it is not, then I need to make some decisions on behalf of the organization right away.

Round 10

Fight or Flight

According to Wikipedia, the fight-or-flight response is a physiological reaction in response to a perceived harmful event, attack, or threat to survival. The response was first described by Walter Bradford Cannon. His theory states that animals react to threats with a general discharge of the sympathetic nervous system, priming the animal for fighting or fleeing.

The sport of boxing has given me one of the most interesting perspectives on this concept. Fighting or fleeing is a principle that is applicable to boxing, business, and life. Having the courage and fortitude to stay in the fight and finish is a trait that builds character. Normalcy has its advantages as we all prefer to live a chaos-free life. However, it is the person in the arena of duress and challenge who learns about life and themselves. We do not prefer the rigors of challenges and dramatic circumstance; however, they are a universal part of life. Witness the fighter who takes a big hit but gets up off the mat to finish the round, the business owner who loses a major account yet continues to press forward and rebuild, or the person who suffers the loss of a family member, friend, or colleague and yet continues to be resilient. These trials are what great principles are built on.

The ability to fight instead of flee when the circumstances aren't in your favor is admirable. We cheer on the underdog who is faced with unfathomable situations. We rave at the process by which the elements of plot are accentuated. We are intrigued by suspense. We respect hard work. And in the end, we see the importance of standing your ground and being a champion. These are the fundamentals of life that boxing has taught me. Whether you are in the boxing ring, the ring of business, or the ring of life, it is a fight. And the variables that influence your response are in many instances the variables that will influence your life.

With all great fighters, there comes a time when the impulse to take flight surfaces. It is in that purgatory moment when a decision has to be made. A key factor in decision-making is discernment and knowing when to walk away. This happened to me when I sustained a career-ending automobile accident. It was a huge blow, and I was catapulted into making a major decision in my life. My passion for boxing was immense, and the mere thought of losing such a precious piece of my life was one of the biggest challenges I'd faced. Should I go back into the ring and continue to fight and take a chance on losing my life, or should I step aside, take flight, and walk away?

Thankfully I made the right decision to move on. That very decision allowed me to become a spokesman for the sport and get involved in other aspects of the boxing world. Had I continued to fight, I may have further injured myself or worse.

In the end, we should be aware of the pros and cons of our lives and make informed, smart, and strategic decisions that are in our best interest. Sometimes they may sting a bit, but it's always best to do what's right. Information, recognition, and acceptance are always good barometers for decision-making.

Round 11

Where Do We Go from Here?

Who really knows where boxing will wind up?

There is good and bad in every aspect of business, sports, and life. Too many promoters out there today really do not care about the fighters. If they truly cared about the fighters, retirement plans would be set up for them, insurance would be provided, and all fighters would have to do is train. That is in the perfect world of this unforgiving sport. I am not saying that every promoter is out just for themselves. Yes, I have worked with some very good promoters around the country over the past several years. They have always been more than fair with the fighters, and I will continue to work with them and try to promote the sport in a very positive way. I have always surrounded myself with good people, and I have worked very hard to create a good name for myself in this business.

Yet it will continue to be an uphill battle for the fighters who fill the pockets of the promoters while trying to work out the best possible deal for themselves in the sport. Not every fighter can become the next Mayweather or De La Hoya. What we are discussing in this book has gone on since the beginnings of boxing. There will always be trainers, managers, and promoters who will take advantage of fighters all over the country and the world until the fighters can unite for a common cause and change the sport. The Mayweathers and the De La Hoyas are the exceptions who have done very well financially over the last several years in our sport that dates back to Roman times. The Ali Act was intended to protect amateur and professional boxers across this country, but since 2002 when the law was put into place, nothing has really been done to improve the sport or the fighters.

As I said earlier, we face an uphill battle to make change happen. How much longer will professional fighters have to wind up broke or destitute on the mean streets of every city across this country due to being taken advantage of by manager, trainer, or promoters whom they fought for?

It really is up to us as former fighters to make sure that this does not happen to the fighters who come after us in the sport. Yes, Senator John McCain of Arizona has helped to create the Muhammad Ali Act, but until people really start to take notice of what goes on behind the scenes, the negative aspects will continue to be covered up and swept under the rug. It is time to educate the fans and the participants so we no longer have to read about ex-fighters living on the streets, barely being able to survive, or going hungry because they were taken advantage of and wound up broke.

I don't know about you, but I would really like not to have to attend another fundraiser because of a fighter being down and out on his luck, only to see the same thing happen over and over again to him or her. The only way to prevent this is by making some serious changes to the sport and how it is overseen.

Round 12

Get in the Fight

Nothing will ever change until young fighters decide to educate themselves and learn the ins and outs of the sport. We have had a century of neglect in the sport; I think that it is time for change. We cannot allow boxing to continue to stand stagnant and not progress for the fighters who make the sport what it is today, or ignore the legacy of the great fighters who paved the way for everyone who is involved in the sport today. Boxing has become big business, and big business brings out the bad guys who see ways to make money through dishonest dealings and taking advantage of the fighters. Education is the key to success and to change.

A level playing field will allow fighters to negotiate fair contracts for themselves along with the help of their trainers or managers. This book is also intended for managers and trainers who once were fighters and wound up in the same situation. It is time to break the mold.

I know that poor treatment of fighters will continue as long as there is no one to oversee those who are in control of the sport today. Write letters to Senator John McCain or even to the federal government and let them know that the Ali Act is being broken and that nothing is being done about it.

It is time to expose all of the laws that are being broken within the sport and to bring these acts to the surface. As I mentioned in the previous chapter, there are good fight promoters out there who do the right thing each and every fight card. They truly care about the fighters and the sport and love what they do. In the end, I hope that this book will help to educate you so that you do not wind up as a statistic like the many fighters who have fought before you in the last one hundred years or so, and that you leave the sport a little better when you retire from it.

The abuses are also happening in other professional sports due to the same lack of education, I hope that I am able to cross the sports barriers with this book and be able to educate professional athletes from other sports here in the USA and abroad.

The Tragic side of boxing

Boxing has to be one of the most loved sports of the world, but there is also a very tragic side to the sport that never is really talked about. Most boxers turn to the sport looking for a way to fight their way off of the mean streets, seeing it as a way to improve their economic status and to make a better way of life for themselves and their families. Over the last several years there have been many tragic deaths of some of the most beloved boxers in the world. Alexis Arguello was found dead in his home town of Managua, Nicaragua on May 5th, 2010, of a self-inflicted gun shot. He was a true champion who was beloved by fans from all over the world. Arturo Gatti was another boxer who was tragically murdered while on vacation in Brazil in 2009, and no one was ever charged with his murder. The police in Brazil called it a suicide, and that was the end of the story.

Diego Corrales was another tragic loss in the boxing world when he was killed while on his motorcycle after being involved in a three-car accident in Las Vegas. Salvador Sanchez perished while driving his Porsche at an excessive rate of speed on a highway in Mexico. The tragedy of the sport seems to be as much a part of the sport as the boxers who fight themselves. Tragedy is a part of the sport, and that will never change; what can change is the education of the participants who are in the sport, so they will be able to walk away and be financially set, or at least have a fighting chance in life. The other thing that needs to be done is to have a medical insurance policy put in place for fighters who fight on any promoter's fight card. It should be made mandatory that fight promoters provide medical insurance for fighters, so that in cases where the fighter is injured, the insurance policy will take care of them and they will not have a financial burden placed on them.

Here is a list of former World Champion Boxers who have went broke and filed for bankruptcy over the years. I have also included a few other professional athletes as examples, because this is not only limited to fighters. Do not allow yourself to become another statistic.

Mike Tyson reportedly earned over 350 Million Dollars earned over his career

Evander Holyfield reportedly 250 Million Dollars earned over his career

Riddick Bowe reportedly earned over 50 Million Dollars over his career

Iran Barkley reportedly earned over 5 Million Dollars earned over his career

Joe Louis reportedly 4.6 Million Dollars earned over his career

Latrell Sprewell, Basketball reportedly earned over 100 Million Dollars

Marion Jones, Track Star, earned $80,000 per race

Antoine Walker, Basketball, reportedly earned over 110 Million Dollars

As you can see, the list of celebrity sports stars who have went broke over the years is amazing, and the list goes on and on. This is being repeated over and over, time and time again. When will it stop? The amount of money that these professional athletes earn is staggering, and they should have never wind up in these dire circumstances. Was it bad decision-making, bad management or not educating themselves, that caused them to wind up in this position? Hopefully this book will help to educate you, so you do not wind up in this position and find yourself Unprotected.

Epilogue

I have been involved with boxing in the USA over the years, managing a few professional boxers and putting on amateur shows and supporting local boxing programs around the city. I was also involved with the World Boxing Hall of Fame as an executive board member. I am currently the North American coordinator for the World Boxing Foundation and former North American coordinator for the World Boxing Federation. These positions have allowed me to travel all over the country and abroad as a supervisor and an international boxing judge.

I will continue to work in this sport for as long as I can to leave my mark in some way on a sport that I truly love and respect. Most importantly, I will help educate and guide boxers and anyone else who has a need and wants to learn no matter what your passion or profession is. I do not want to hear of another boxer, professional athlete, or businessperson who has been taken advantage of just because he or she failed to educate himself or herself in the world of business or with good life skills.

Every day brings a new challenge in our lives, no matter what profession we are in, be it sports, business, or being an employee. It is never too late to learn or to apply your knowledge and skills to succeed and get ahead in life.

Challenge yourself each and every day to learn something new, because we never ever stop learning unless we choose to do so. The human mind is powerful, and it can absorb as much knowledge as you can feed it. Never ever stop learning, for it is the power of learning that will help you travel down your path to success.

Questions for Review

1. When was boxing introduced to the United States, and by whom?

2. What year was amateur boxing first introduced into the Olympics?

3. Name one reason that you want to read through your contract before signing it.

4. What is the purpose of a manager?

5. How many weight classes are there in professional boxing?

6. What is the promoter's job?

7. Who is the greatest boxer of all time?

8. What do you need to do in order to become a licensed professional boxer?

9. How many rounds do amateur boxers fight and what is the length of the round?

10. Can you fight without a license, professionally or as an amateur?

11. Why is the Ali Act important to boxers?

12. Who oversees amateur boxing in the USA?

13. Why is a contract important to you as a professional athlete?

14. What do you need to have in order to open up a bank account?

15. Can an individual resister his name as a DBA?

16. Are you responsible for taxes on any money that you earn as a professional boxer?

17. What are the responsibilities of a trainer?

18. Is a physical necessary in order to compete in a boxing match?

19. Who oversees professional boxing here in the USA?

20. How many weight classes are there in professional boxing?

Notes

Index

About the Author

Alan Santana

A resounding, gregarious personality is an immediate characteristic that exudes Alan Santana. The fanatical ringside commentator extols an arsenal of burlesque, intelligence, and accuracy that is adored by his many fans. A mutlitalented commentator, speaker, and serial entrepreneur presiding as the North American Coordinator for the World Boxing Foundation, the California native is one of the most experienced and knowledgeable experts of our time. He has held the position of Executive Board Member with the World Boxing Hall of Fame, International Boxing Judge, and his appointment to these positions has led to an array of opportunities in the boxing world.

Santana began boxing at eight years old, and it grew into a twenty-year career. He earned a spot as a member of the California/ USA Boxing Team from 1982 to 1985. During his amateur stint, he won many state and local titles and recorded well over 100-plus fights. Shortly after starting his professional run, his career was unexpectedly hampered due to sustaining a career-ending injury from an automobile accident. Santana continues his support of the coveted sport of boxing through national and international travel supervising title bouts as a champion of the sport and a passionate mentor to youth.

He currently presides as the CEO, President, and Founder of No Teen Riders, INC., a nonprofit organization created to educate teen drivers and their families by providing practical information, preventive measures, and compliance standards to reduce and eliminate teen vehicular deaths. Alan resides in Orange County, California, and is married to his wife, Annamarie, for over twenty-nine years. They have four children, Victoria; twins, Austin and Andrew; and Aaron.

CPSIA information can be obtained
at www.ICGtesting.com
Printed in the USA
BVHW031301080322
630912BV00004B/54